The Unification of America

I0449332

Edited by Rainer Shea & Gloria Malone

By Santiago Romero©

Table of Contents

Preamble

Simon Bolivar's[1] and Thomas Jefferson's[2] warnings ring louder and clearer now than ever. The defeat of 20th Century Socialism has reduced the American realm into a battlefield. Cities throughout the continent have become gladiator arenas full of competing gangs, drug lords, and human traffickers at the service of decaying capitalism. Locales such as Los Angeles, Miami, New York, Chicago, San Juan, Santo Domingo, Kingston, Mexico City, Rio de Janeiro, Bogota, and many more have become dominated by pimps, thugs, and thieves working in service of multinational land developers, foreign investors, comprador capitalists, agribusiness giants, real estate moguls, offshore banks, etc. The politicians who allow such robbery and misery to the working classes are all on their payroll. The Capitalist efforts to refeudalize[3] the American continent as a whole has led to the criminalization of the peoples who inhabit the Western Hemisphere, from Hudson Bay to the Strait of Magellan. In response to an increase in crime, deindustrialization, unemployment, prostitution, and disease, a growing number of laboring and oppressed people are confronting the neo-colonial[4] hegemony with the aim of abolishing this geo-political parasite.

It's high time that a hemispheric-wide, Pan-American Revolution against capitalism and imperialism swallows the continent as a whole, from Hawaii and California to Puerto Rico and Boston, from Anchorage and Montreal to Buenos Aires and Caracas. Only then can the colonized and working peoples be liberated from the yolk of western imperialism, remnants of caste society, and the psychological grip of superstition, both catholic and evangelical. The only cure for the damage caused by the profit incentive is a Socialist Revolution, which will lead to the development of Communism.

I.   A Class Analysis of American Society

When one thinks of American society, images of burgers and football come to mind. They also think of rock music and the Statue of Liberty. Not only that, but they also think of Hollywood and fifty stars and thirteen stripes. In short, America is often conflated with the United States. This is no further from the truth; America is neither a nation nor civilization, but rather a collection of them across the hemisphere. Allowing this obfuscation to continue further cements the North American monopoly over the rest of the continent for the following reasons: a) it gives the United States a de facto monopoly on a term that applies to the nations south of the Rio Grande; b) it prevents transnational working-class unification between Northern, Central, and Southern America by solidifying a culture of US "exceptionalism". This misuse of wording has confused the struggle for the emancipation of American labor - but where does this reckless sloganeering come from? The historic contradiction facing the nations of the Americas' is one between caste and class in both their merger and opposition to each other.

The origin of today's economic development in America isn't rooted in the penetration of European capital investments, colonizing settlers, or the civilizing effect of the church. In all actuality, the origin of today's Greater American economy is rooted in the agrarian settlements which predate the intrusion of European migration and colonization for thousands of years. Another fact worth noting is that America had agriculture hundreds, if not thousands of years before the first farm was established on the European continent. Comrade Roxanne Dunbar Ortiz wrote in her groundbreaking text, *An Indigenous People's History of the United States*[5]:

> "As a birthplace of agriculture and the towns and cities that followed, America is ancient, not a "new world." Domestication of plants took place

around the globe in seven locales during approximately the same period, around 8500 BC. Three of the seven were in the Americas, all based on corn: the Valley of Mexico and Central America (Mesoamerica); the South-Central Andes; and Eastern North America. . . . Only in the American continent was the parallel domestication of animals eschewed in favor of game management, a kind of animal husbandry different from that developed in Africa and Asia."

(Roxanne Dunbar Ortiz; *An Indigenous People's History of the United States.*, Pgs. 15-16)

Why is it that animal husbandry took on a different form in the Americas than throughout the rest of the world? It's due to the fact that resources weren't depleted and were limited in the Americas. Due to its geographic isolation and bountiful resources in comparison to Eurasia and Africa, many Amerindian societies were able to develop use-based economies. To simply put it, the effects of drought, mass flooding, and disease which plagued the "Old World" hadn't affected America on a mass scale until the arrival of colonizing forces. Therefore, the development of centralized States wasn't fairly common, although Amerindian civilizations typically had more equity and protocols. Bear in mind that as of 2016, five of the top fifteen nations with the most arable land are all located in the Americas according to the *CIA World Factbook*[6]. Why does this matter? Because environmental factors didn't cause endless warfare, mass migration, or conflict between pastoralists and agrarian settlements on the scale that it did elsewhere due to pastoralism being virtually nonexistent; the latter had virtually no competition with the former in pre-contact America[7].

Hemispheric-wide trading was also developed in America on a scale not even seen in Eurasia until much later. The Arawakan language family has way more diversity than the Romance dialects[8]. This linguistic lineage at its height spanned from Florida and the Caribbean to Peru and Brazil. The Uto-Aztecan language family during the pre-contact period stems from Southern Mexico to the Northern interior

4

of the United States. The Na-Dene language family touches nearly all of Alaska with offshoots in the South of Texas and New Mexico. In school, American children are typically taught, especially in the reactionary States of the continent, that it was Europeans who brought trade to the Western Hemisphere. Archeological evidence shows that this isn't the case[9]:

> "Indigenous agriculture was based on corn. Traces of cultivated corn have been identified in Central Mexico dating back ten thousand years. Twelve to fourteen centuries later, corn production had spread throughout the temperate and tropical Americas from the southern tip of South America to the subarctic of North America, and from the Pacific to the Atlantic Ocean on both continents. . . . Unlike most grains, corn cannot grow wild and cannot exist without attentive human care.
>
> Along with multiple varieties and colors of corn, Mesoamericans cultivated squash and beans, which were extended throughout the hemisphere, as were the many varieties and colors of potato cultivated by Andean farmers more than 7,000 years ago. Corn, being a summer crop, can tolerate no more than 30 days without water and even less in high temperatures. Many of the areas where corn was the staple were arid or semiarid, so its cultivation required the design and construction of complex irrigation systems - in place at least two thousand years before Europeans knew the Americas existed. The proliferation of agriculture and cultigens could not have occurred without centuries of cultural and commercial interchange among the peoples of North, Central and South America, whose traders carried seeds as well as other goods and cultural practices."

(Ibid., Pg. 16)

As noted by Peruvian Marxist Jose Carlos Mariategui in his work *Seven Interpretive Essays on Peruvian Reality*[10]:

> "The degree to which the history of Peru was severed by the conquest can be seen better on an economic than on any other level. Here the conquest most clearly appears to be a break in continuity. Until the conquest, an economy developed in Peru that sprang spontaneously and freely from the Peruvian

soil and people. The most interesting aspect of the empire of the Incas, which was a grouping of agricultural and sedentary communities, was its economy. All historical evidence agrees that the Inca people—industrious, disciplined, pantheist, and simple—lived in material comfort. With abundant food their population increased. The Malthusian problem was completely unknown to the empire. Although the collectivist organization directed by the Incas had weakened the Indians' individual initiative, it had instilled in them the habit of a humble and religious obedience to social duty, which benefitted the economic system. The Incas derived as much social utility as possible from this trait. They improved the vast Inca territory by constructing roads, canals, et cetera, and they extended its borders by conquering nearby tribes. Collective work and common effort were employed fruitfully for social purposes."

(Jose Carlos Mariategui; *Seven Interpretive Essays on Peruvian Reality.,* Pg. 7)

The only thing the European crowns did for the Americas in terms of trade was to link the already established trade networks of the Amerindians with that of Eurasia, Africa, and Oceania. Furthermore, the rapid economic development of the Americas wouldn't have found suit if there wasn't an already established agrarian base that predates all commercial activity. Before there can be manufacturing or commodity production of any kind, there has to be a consistent supply of food to aid in the procreation and survival of the workforce. It's no coincidence that Europe's feudal economic model was able to take firm root in the Americas within a few generations. This is in stark contrast to the several hundreds of years in the case of European feudalism after the fall of the Roman Empire. If anything, European colonization stunted trade development in the Americas as Criollos, Mestizos, and Amerindians alike were unable to trade outside of their colonial boundaries.

With European powers in competition with each other over how to divide the world, American civilization both pre-and even post-contact was parasitically destroyed. Or it was scaled back in order to provide

Europe with the resources it needed to develop its economies and militaries with world-conquering capabilities. How was this mass destruction of entire nations and nationalities possible?

It started off at the familial level through the creation and/or intensification of a racial caste system to prevent another Bacon's Rebellion[11] from rocking the entire hemisphere. By dividing the laboring masses with a color line, whether it be against Amerindians who still largely populated what is now considered Latin America, or stratifying the enslaved African diaspora which replaced the former wherever they were wiped out.

However, in cohesion with establishing the color line, the demarcation between males and females on the American continent began as Europe sought to consolidate its economic model upon the American continent. Why so? Because the economic model of the Old World (not exclusively Europe) is highly dependent on the woman being reduced to a housewife. The native women in America could no longer wield the same socio-political power they had prior to when Columbus landed in the "New World." Adding the nail to the coffin of Amerindian civilization was the enforced shift from matrilineal to patrilineal inheritance - solidifying male supremacy and ensuring female subordination. As noted by Howard Zinn in his groundbreaking work, *A People's History of the United States,* he repeats La Casas's description of pre-contact Amerindian civilization[12]:

> "Marriage laws are non-existent: men and women alike choose their mates and leave them as they please, without offense, jealousy or anger."

> (Howard Zinn; *A People's History of the United States.,* Pg. 5)

Through the influx of impoverished migrants from Europe, oftentimes persecuted religious communities, along with implementing "divide and conquer" tactics setting male against female, settler against colonized, etc, Europe was able to successfully recreate America in its image. Feudalism replaced the collectivist societies of the Amerindians. Male domination replaced equality between the sexes. Urban crime, in conjunction with economic exploitation, increased with a stark rise in prostitution, the distribution of contraband, and thievery. Nature went from being a shared and respected force to becoming an unstable servant. Societies that cultivated a wide variety of foodstuffs had their soil reduced to a mono-crop quality, one in which only a single type of plant, often a cash crop, is suitable for cultivation. This was, thanks in part, to careless extensive agriculture on the part of the colonizing powers without using the crop rotation methods employed in Europe.

It was centuries of colonial oppression and de-development which caused the new merchant classes, many of whom were criollo, to rebel against their respective European crowns. Such was the case in the American Revolutionary War or the South American wars of independence. Many of the leaders of these respective revolutions were former colonial overseers faced with overthrow if they didn't make concessions to the merchants, mestizos, mulattos, maroons, and Amerindians who comprised the bulk of the agrarian workforce. This was also the case in the Cuban, Haitian, and Mexican wars for independence. When push comes to shove, an empty stomach sounds the same regardless of sex or nationality.

However, what replaced colonialism wasn't the "free and open democracy," but rather a neo-colonial arrangement protected by a liberal-conservative order in which ALL of the wealthy had a say-so. Unlike its predecessor colonialism, neo-colonialism wasn't protected by a monarch, but by a plutocracy working in favor of private interests rather than that of a particular royal family. Why does this matter? It's due to the fact that although on one hand, the productive backwardness and slow economic growth which plagued the feudal model were replaced by a more efficient mode of production, on the other hand it diversified privilege and imperial expansion. In the old days, only those born into a bloodline "ordained by God" could wield command over an empire. Now anyone with a large sum of capital, regardless of hereditary lineage, could be selected into their nation's parliaments as the representative of the corporations. What replaced political aristocracy was monopoly capitalism.

Many countries have either fallen victim to, or flat-out embraced, the neo-colonial model. The states of Northern America (the USA and Canada) became neo-colonial powers, with Central and Southern America (the Dominican Republic and Peru) becoming their puppets. Instead of using firepower in the initial assault upon a fledgling nation, the neo-colonial powers used the export of their financial capital to take over weaker economies for pennies on the peso. On paper, many of these nations were "independent" and "self-reliant." Historical reality paints a completely different picture. How can a nation be independent when its economy is owned by foreign investors with their subsidiaries lobbying their politicians - flooding their election campaigns with large reserves of capital investment? In return, these politicians arrange "defense" and "trade" agreements that operate in favor of the imperialist states of North America and Europe.

Yet there's another detail to take into account. This detail was noted by the late Comrade Kwame Nkrumah, who pointed out that the practice of neo-colonialism, like its predecessor colonialism, is designed to transfer the problems of the more developed nations to that of the peripheral nations. Yet, he also pointed out how it's different in the sense that[13]:

> "The introduction of neo-colonialism increases the rivalry between the great powers which was provoked by the old-style colonialism. However little real power the government of a neo-colonialist State may possess, it must have, from the very fact of its nominal independence, a certain area of manoeuvre. It may not be able to exist without a neo-colonialist master but it may still have the ability to change masters."

(Kwame Nkrumah; *Neocolonialism: The Highest Stage of Imperialism.*, Pg. xiv)

How does this play into today's class dynamic in the continent? It's simple: there are two variations of the same classes, with the periphery classes being universal. In understanding the historical development of these contending classes, each vying for their supremacy, are we able to understand what role the progressive classes play and how they are to play that role? Part of comprehending this is being able to understand the importance of the late Comrade Mao Tse-Tung's words in his essay *Analysis of the Classes in Chinese Society*[14]:

> "Who are our enemies? Who are our friends? This is a question of the first importance for the revolution. . . . To ensure that we will definitely achieve success in our revolution and will not lead the masses astray, we must pay attention to uniting with our real friends in order to attack our real enemies. To distinguish real friends from real enemies, we must make a general analysis of the economic status of the various classes. . ."

(Mao Tse-Tung; *Selected Works Vol. I.*, Pg. 13)

Within the American context, this analysis must have a two-fold nature, given the respectively different historical conditions for the economic base of all of the Americas. What replaced chattel slavery and the caste system in Northern and Southern America became, through the push and pull struggle between downtrodden and privileged, a soft form of apartheid enforced through hereditary laws regarding property - the biggest one being an inheritance. Inheritance determines the position that someone has more so in the Americas than in Europe. This is due to the fact that incentives to loot wealth from the Amerindian population along with the trans-Atlantic slave trade have elevated the status of a sizable minority of the hemisphere, mostly settlers or criollos, though this category includes other nationalities as well. All while centuries of slavery and exploitation have stunted the development of Mestizos, Mullatos, Maroons, Amerindians, and rural Whites.

The first classes are the capitalist classes.

In America, these classes work in unison to secure their monopoly over the markets of the western hemisphere. The **imperial capitalists** are a capitalist class that exports the finance capital (with the protection of NATO military power) to the Third World in order to dominate a smaller nation's domestic economy by dictating production. The **comprador capitalists**, a capitalist class based in the neo-colonial puppet state, is tasked with overseeing and implementing the policies determined by the imperial capitalists. These classes are enemy number one.

The second classes are the proletarian class.

In America, these classes are often set up against each other by the capitalists in order to keep them from recognizing that they all play a key role in the transcontinental economy of the Americas. Production has been linked continent-wide. To prevent continental working class unity, the capitalist classes created two distinctive variations of the proletariat within this hemispheric order. The first distinction is the **proletariat**, the industrial working class, themselves. They occupy the Northern portion of our hemisphere and are growing in the Southern portion as well, primarily in the metropole. The second distinction is the **semi-proletariat**, a proletariat in transition from another class. In the Americas, the bulk of this class works in agriculture. This class is the main focus and ally of the revolution.

The dominant periphery class is the **lumpen-proletariat**, the millions of prostitutes, underemployed, unemployed, homeless, drug dealers, and thieves. This class is extremely dangerous and volatile. Although it faces the most violent forms of state repression, it's because of its lack of a **proletarian conscience**, and the focus on being productive and victorious against capitalism, that its members are easily swayed into being the foot soldiers of finance capital. This especially happens with gang members. In Sanyika Shakur's book, *MONSTER: The Autobiography of an L.A. Gang Member,* his analysis of street gangs arrives at a highly militaristic, hyper-patriarchal conclusion which focuses on firepower rather than political development[15]:

> "There is troop movement throughout the city, in some areas the fighting is intense. The soldiers are engaged in a "civil war." A war without terms. A war fought by any means necessary, with anything at their disposal. . . .
> . . . Neither side receives funding from any government, nor does either side claim any allegiance to any particular religion or socioeconomic system of government. There are no representatives from either faction in the United Nations, nor does either side recognize the Universal Declaration of Human Rights."
>
> (Sanyika Shakur; *MONSTER: The Autobiography of an L.A. Gang Member.*, Pgs. xi-xii.)

How do hereditary-based property laws play into this? A few things must be taken into consideration.

Felons often face housing discrimination and aren't approved for homes or jobs, even if they meet the qualifications for said housing or employment. This leads many felons to be stuck in economically precarious situations due to increased difficulty of acquiring a successful reintegration into mainstream society. In a study conducted by the *National Institute of Justice*, evidence shows that the United States has a recidivism rate of forty-four percent[16]. It's no coincidence that with the United States having the highest incarceration rate, up to 80 percent of prisoners grew up in single-parent households, almost all of them led by a woman[17]. This is caused by the elites setting men and women against each other in order to destroy the working class family.

The conclusion of this class analysis leads the revolutionary masses to understand how the merger of the feudal hereditary caste, and the economically determined class, has intensified the process of refeudalization in both Northern and Southern America. The proliferation and reproduction of semi-feudal conditions has resulted in the medievalization of the Americas. Forced labor has been disguised as convict "rehabilitation." The Trans-Atlantic slave trade has been replaced with an influx of migrant labor by the same capitalists who destroyed their home countries in the first plac. The solidification of political and economic aristocracies as monopoly capitalism leads to the centralization of state power, in reflection of the centralization of production and commerce. Only a proletarian revolution can resolve this contradiction.

II.   Pink Tide, Red Wave: The Continental Workers' Struggle

The lessons of 20th Century Socialism have taught the working classes when and where to play capitalism as to beat it at its own game, and when and where to play Socialism as to establish infrastructural development. These two games are part of a bigger task of consolidating a foundation of *economic patriotism*, or Socialism. *Economic patriotism* is needed in a world where multinational capitalists and imperialist powers are saber-rattling in their quest for resources. For *economic patriotism* to work, there must be transnational cooperation within the region guaranteeing it won't be isolated into capitulation through siege and sanction. This transnational cooperation will steer the international working classes into a global assault upon capitalism. This was the case with the Soviets answering the Eurasian question, or with today's China enriching its neighbors through its *Belt and Road Initiative*[18]. It's clear as day that the continental workers' struggle is the link between proletarian patriotism and proletarian internationalism.

    The economic developments of the 20th century have resulted in a merger of Latin and Anglo America. Especially after the Spanish-American war, where the United States was able to assert its geopolitical dominance over Latin America after defeating a fledgling Spain. From that point on, the Monroe Doctrine became the de-facto ideology of the United States. This development, along with the destabilization of Latin American countries with war debt owed to the United States and Western Europe from their crusades for independence from Spain, have caused crime, poverty, and mass migration all throughout the hemisphere. Consequently, not only has the migration from Latin American countries introduced an influx of Spanish speakers into the United States, merging the Anglo and Latin realms.

But the existence of Quebec and Arcadia within the country of Canada is another, lesser-known example of this cultural heterogeneity. Mass deportations of US-born nationals to their ancestral homes in Latin America have notably increased the number of English speakers in the southern portion of the hemisphere.

With the immigration industry in collusion with industrial capitalism creating an influx of semi-proletarians living in serf-like conditions has begun the refeudalization of the United States and even Canada. The United States, and increasingly the Canadian economy as well, cannot function without a large supply of cheap labor imported from the Third World, especially places within Latin America and the Caribbean[19]. This became a clause for the continual destabilization of Latin America in the later stage of the Cold War, carried out on behalf of North American imperialists. In order to prevent Socialistic and Communistic sympathies present in Latin America from reaching north of the Rio Grande, the Reagan administration in the 1980s began working hand in hand with drug traffickers, human smugglers, and right-wing paramilitaries in wrecking progressive and revolutionary projects throughout the region. On the other hand, the economies of North America were struggling to find a new source of cheap labor, since the North American worker in the eyes of the capitalists was expecting "too much". This alternative workforce was to live in dirt poor conditions, be terribly paid, and coerced into doing whatever their "sponsor" demanded of them. The Trans-Atlantic Slave Trade was replaced with the modern-day immigration industry - those worthy of citizenship were granted asylum, while those deemed unworthy of citizenship were dished out indentured servitude.

As the labor pools of Northern and Southern America became more and more fused into one, there began a noticeable decline in living standards. The United States and Canada have been witness to jingoistic anti-immigration and xenophobic propaganda, which has turned members of the laboring classes against each other on the basis of their skin tone and language. The complexities of the Latin American caste system, and the need to diversify the privileges granted to oppressed nationalities to maintain their social stratification, have made this basis even more-so blurred. With a noticeable demographic decline of the white population, many fascist ideologues and movements have been relaxing the definition of whiteness as a means to recruit more people into their ranks, the first in line being white Latinos. With North American-dominated capitalism undergoing an identity crisis, the Socialist Pink Tide across the Americas has re-established and reinvented the national identities of previously bullied and defeated countries[20].

This anti-imperialist struggle must be linked with the anti-colonial struggles inside the United States imperial proper, as well as with the Canadian question. This is the only sure way to victory in the American hemisphere. This has historically been the case as imperialism and neo-colonialism have ravaged nations throughout the world in barbaric conquest and exploitation; causing many of the peripheral countries to add fuel to the fire on the very same problems as the ones within the imperial core. Problems which were exported to the undeveloped nations of the world. As noted by Comrade Stalin in *The Foundations of Leninism*[21]:

> "The third contradiction is the contradiction between the handful of ruling "civilized" nations and the hundreds of millions of the colonial and dependent peoples of the world. Imperialism is the most barefaced exploitation and the most inhumane oppression of hundreds of millions of people inhabiting vast colonies and dependent countries.
> The growth of revolutionary movement in all colonies and dependent countries without exception clearly testifies to this fact. This circumstance is of importance for the proletariat in that it radically undermines the position of capitalism by converting the colonies and dependent countries from reserves of imperialism into reserves of the proletarian revolution."

(Joseph Stalin: *The Foundations of Leninism*; Pg. 6)

This solution will naturally lead to Pan-Americanism. Why Pan-Americanism? Because imperialism is both a symptom of societal unrest in civilized countries, and of backwardness in the peripheral countries. How so? It's due to the fact that problems in the imperial countries become so bad that many within these countries begin to revolt. Which makes the capitalists provide concessions. To pay for these concessions, the imperialists set up puppet governments in the peripheral countries to secure investments. For this reason, Comrade Fidel Castro noted that[22]:

> "The drawing together of the revolutionaries of the United States with those of Latin America is the most natural thing in the world, and the most spontaneous."

(Fidel Castro; *Fidel Castro Reader.*, Pg. 293)

Pan-American sentiments are routinely expressed by the progressive governments of Latin America which have broken free from North American imperialism and neocolonialism. Pioneer Hugo Chavez of Venezuela established Pan-American alliances to solidify Latin American control over its own resources. His successor, Nicolas Maduro along with Evo Morales of Bolivia, have also expressed sympathy for Latin American cooperation. This is especially true of AMLO of Mexico, Daniel Ortega of Nicaragua, and the Kirchners in Argentina.

Yet Pan-Americanism on its own isn't enough. The economic problems facing the progressive developments in Latin America are caused by remaining capitalistic structures that are still in place. These countries have capitalist ruling classes that are still in power. In the progressive countries of Latin America, the patriotic and class struggles have not been completed. This is due to the sanctioning and sieging effect of North American imperialism, especially that of the United

States. In order to aid these progressive developments, there must be a revolutionary development in the United States and Canada, the imperial core. Such a development will lead to socialism, or *economic patriotism,* to make things simpler[23].

This pink tide must be turned burgundy red in a struggle to establish Socialism and Communism across the Americas. Is it not only right that the working classes are in power? Is not only right that state machinery rigged against the toilers be turned on its head, and utilized against the exploiters? Why not equality between big business and organized labor? It's due to the contradictions between the two being so acute that there can be no respite till one reigns supreme. Every time the working classes try to establish better conditions for themselves, it's met with the harshest reprisals. "Counter-terrorism" measures such as union busting, right wing death squads, assassinations of intellectuals and activists, the slaughter of clergy and indigenous *Campesinos*, etc[24]. It's only right that the working classes not only put a halt to the harshest retaliatory efforts by the ruling classes, but halt the ruling classes' efforts to acquire political power and accumulate capital.

The day when the working class accomplishes both of these tasks is soon to arrive. Sooner than one may consider. We're on the eve of when revolution sweeps the entire hemisphere, and embroils the continent as a whole into a full-fledged *proletarian revolution*. After the seizure of state power in the North American states, the following program must be installed:

1. The United States and Canada exiting NATO, the IMF, and other military, political, and economic alliances with capitalist states.

2. The sublation of the United States and Canada into a People's Federation of America with independence and autonomy granted to its internal colonies[25]

3. The reunification of Aztlan with the rest of Mexico, along with joining the People's Federation of America[26]

4. The capital of the People's Federation of America is to be located in Chicago, since it's a city near the center of North America. This guarantees more efficient territorial administration. Chicago is to be jointly claimed and administered by the independent states of the People's Federation of America.

5. The expansion of jointly claimed territorial administrations (federation districts) in key commercial, environmental, and cultural areas, as a means of preventing balkanization, or the break up of the federation

6. The nationalization of all banking, heavy and light industries, and agriculture. This policy is to be enacted continent-wide.

7. The end of private home ownership in order to pave the way for personal home ownership. Along with vehicles and other necessary items needed for life.

8. Free education (including secondary) and healthcare for all citizens of the People's Federation of America.

9. The establishment of a *Women's Revolutionary Legal Code.* Such a legal code gives women, by mandate, equal and fair representation in the People's Federation of America.

10. The harmonious merger of ecological economics, industrial development, and scientific incentives to safeguard a healthy, prosperous future for everybody.

In understanding the objective of Pan-American Socialism, it's crucial to note that only through a hemisphere-wide unification of the anti-imperialist struggles along with that of the labor movement will the workers of the Americas be able to establish continental *economic patriotism* or socialism.

As it stands, the popular and progressive governments of Latin America are in a territorial crosshair known as dual-power. To turn this crosshair into a blitzkrieg against finance capital across the whole continent, revolutionary momentum must be introduced to the northern portion of the hemisphere, and it already has. Such a victory will help the American worker of all nationalities establish a Dictatorship of the Proletariat, or a worker-controlled democracy. Or as Comrade Mao Tse-Tung put it[27]:

> "The people's democratic dictatorship uses two methods. Towards the enemy, it uses the method of dictatorship, that is, for as long a period of time as is necessary it does not let them take part in political activities and compels them to obey the law of the People's Government and to engage in labor, and through labor, transform themselves into new men. Towards the people, on the contrary, it uses the method not of compulsion but of democracy, that is, it must necessarily let them take part in political activities and does not compel them to do this or that, but uses the method of democracy in educating and persuading them"

> (Mao Tse-Tung; *Closing speech at the Second Session of the First National Committee of the Chinese People's Political Consultative Conference;* June 23, 1950)

III. Ideological Trends in the American Socialist Movement

Postmodern capitalism has morphed the definitions of right and wrong, ignorant and wise, civilized and barbaric. This economic (mis) arrangement is also responsible, with the help of social media platforms controlled by multinational corporations with state department contracts, for changing and incorrectly rewriting the definition of socialism. This revisioning is nothing new, but it's more intensified today than ever due to the expanded usage of the fascist states' psychological warfare mechanisms. This has produced multitudes of fraudulent "socialist" schools of thought, some new, others dating back to the days of Marx and Engels themselves. The following outlines the material conditions that have given rise to the schools of socialist thought in the Americas.

a. Counter-Revolutionary Socialism

Social Democracy

Social democracy, or "socialism" through reform, is the most pernicious enemy of the revolutionary movement. It confuses the masses and corrals them into being shock troops for the liberal establishment. Today they like to call themselves "democratic socialists". These include types such Bernie Sanders and Alexandria Ocasio Cortez. They preach power to the people, while supporting imperialist aggression against working people worldwide. This contributes to the refugee crisis at the Southern border of the United States, and to the internal migration crisis within North America as a whole. Social democracy is the safeguard of these conditions, since it never addresses the root, but mitigates (temporarily) the problem by minor concessions. This protects the status quo from turmoil for the time being. Overall, social democracy is the belief that somebody can coat themselves in honey, head into a red ant hill, and not get bit.

Historically, social democracy has always been the gateway to fascism. What is fascism? It's a state of emergency led by finance capital to incorporate anti-communism into the administrative apparatus in response to a failed or suppressed workers' movement. Mussolini came into office after the peasant revolts of the agrarian north, and after the workers' upsurge in urban centers was suppressed by his blackshirts operating in the interest of the bourgeois Italian state. Hitler ascended to power years after the Spartacus League was defeated, along with the short-lived Bavarian Soviet Republic. Where do social democrats fall into this? What they do is defang and declaw the labor movement, removing its backbone, its fighting capabilities reduced from that of a tiger to that of a kitten. Through temporary reforms demilitarizing the revolutionary movement, once the capitalist crisis strips away the gains made by the proletariat and semi-proletarian classes, the working classes are left vulnerable to fascism and to fascist leaders.

Where does North America fall into this? The United States and Canada became fascist during the periods between and immediately after the World Wars. They both did so under liberal administrations. Especially in the United States during the 1930s, when FDR's New Deal defanged most of the North American labor movement along with its Communist movement.[28]

Contrary to what many think, fascism isn't just deregulation and refeudalization (at least at first), it can also implement economic planning and welfare state policies. Fascism is flexible like a serpent, reptilic in nature, with its cold-blooded policies luring its prey using a rattle and pacifying it with venom prior to consumption. More often than not, fascism works by appearing more reasonable than previously thought to the average middle-class person. Whenever fascism is thought to be "too-liberal," it shows that it can "stick to its conservative roots." On the contrary, fascism can also enact a left-leaning policy to come off as a movement whose leaders are willing to "negotiate" with "violent leftists" and "union thugs."

Why does this matter? Because an incorrect analysis of fascism leads to the incorrect implementation of tactics, errors in strategic planning, and an unclear goal on behalf of many organizations claiming to possess the "truth" or "formula." This holds much weight given the continual situation of the spontaneous upsurges in the imperial core. Such a failure to analyze the material conditions of North American civilization can prove fatal during periods of fascism. As the late Comrade George Jackson put it:[29]

> "One has to understand that the fascist arrangement tolerates the existence of *no valid* revolutionary activity. It has programmed into its very nature a massive, complex and automatic defense mechanism for all our old methods of raising the consciousness of a potentially revolutionary class of people. The essence of a U.S.A. totalitarian socio-political capitalism is concealed behind the illusion of mass participatory society"

(George Jackson; *Blood In My Eye.*, Pg. 138)

As we stand now, the Biden administration, which was voted in on the supposed foundation of antifascism, is the epitome of fascism itself. Especially given its funding of neo-Nazi Ukraine, which is carrying out a genocidal war against its Russian-speaking eastern regions. On the platform of securing immigrant rights, pictures of mounted border guards whipping Haitian migrants have gone viral, all under Biden's administration. Yet it isn't really his administration, but that of finance capital. Biden is conducting a scorched earth policy throughout the world on a level that makes Trump look like a peacemaker. He came in promising reform, and instead initiated a program of reaction and austerity.

Ultra Leftism

Another variation of counter-revolutionary "socialism" is ultra-leftism. This tendency is the brain rot of the petit-bourgeoisie, and of the lumpen proletarians who provide them with drugs and sexual labor. It's the collapse of revolutionary discipline driven by western degenerate ideals such as free "love," liberation through intoxication, neglect of physical health, in the name of "body positivity," the promotion of plastic surgery in the name of "female empowerment," and the fetishization of violence in the name of "accelerating the revolution." Party and organizational meetings become social clubs full of pornographic idiots who can't put the booze down and keep their noses clean. This is true among the western left, especially in micro-organizations. But it also manifests in the broader mainstream "communist" parties. Ultra-leftism is a petite-bourgeoise trend in the form of outbursts that are completely ignorant of the masses, and that are willing to sacrifice the labor movement to satisfy this unrealistic demand.

Ultra-leftism is the purest form of idealistic, irrational thinking. A revolution is a planned, coordinated series of events that, if applied properly, is to secure the state mechanism for the working class so it can dismantle and reinvent it for the purpose of the revolutionary masses. There's a time and place for everything, especially in a revolution. There will be times when parliamentary methods are needed. There will also be times when the method of struggle must be *outside the box* and where *waters must be tested.* Ultra-leftism dismisses the crucial element of patience to obtain an unobtainable victory through a series of fruitless attempts. In Comrade Lenin's denouncement of the "Social-Revolutionary Party," whose modern equivalent is ANTIFA, he points out that:[30]

". . this party considered itself to be particularly "revolutionary," of "Left,"
because of its recognition of individual terror, assassination - a thing we
Marxists emphatically rejected. Of course, we rejected individual terror only
on the grounds of expediency. . ."

(Vladimir Lenin, *Left Wing Communism: An Infantile Disorder*., Pg. 20)

Ultra-leftism has many faces. In the days of the old, it was
Trotskyism. Now it's Maoism. Anarchism has always been a
counter-revolutionary threat. The leaders of these ideologies claim to be
the most principled arbiters of "socialism," yet invariably they betray
the revolution; Trotsky, for instance, wanted to sell his native Ukraine
to Hitler, despite being Jewish himself. The distorters of Chairman Mao
Tse-Tung bombed labor organizers in the name of fighting "government
infiltration" in Peru. The anarchists led under Nestor Makhno raped and
pillaged the countryside in the name of fighting Soviet
"Authoritarianism." It's highly imperative that this tendency is to be
combatted within and outside our ranks on every front - ideologically,
and if necessary, physically.

b. Progressive Socialism

Socialism of the 21st Century

In the year 1999, Hugo Chavez came into power in Venezuela, forever
changing its history and that of Latin America. Under his terms of
service, he reinvented the nation from a plutocracy into an example of
progressive populism. His programs included expanded public housing,
free healthcare, direct democracy, and cultural programs for
Afro-Venezuelans and those of Amerindian descent. He coined the term
Socialism of the 21st Century, meaning a type of socialism adjusted for
the time period of unipolar world domination led by the United States.
This type of socialism includes policies that are severely more lenient

than those of its 20th Century predecessor. This policy of building a popular grassroots movement, yet not achieving complete state power due to economic leniency, has consolidated within the country what has historically been known as dual-power. Venezuela has contending administrations - that of the legitimate president Nicolas Maduro, and that of saboteur Juan Guaido.

This trend of push and pull between exploited and exploiter has spread and continued throughout the Latin American world. Ecuador has witnessed victory and defeat in terms of dealing with the IMF. Argentina has been increasingly recalcitrant against US imperialism as the People's Republic of China becomes its largest trading partner. Evo Morales was overthrown by a counter-revolutionary coup, but his successor toppled the coup of the comprador-bourgeoisie and resolidified popular rule. Nicaragua and Mexico have also joined in on the Pan-American pink tide towards establishing Latin American unity against North American imperialism. In the event of being victorious in this political push and pull, these nations end up getting hit with the most brutal sanctions. Although going all the way in terms of socialist development will further isolate these administrations, it's up to North American anti-imperialists to consolidate the labor movement into one cohesive force against fascism.

Movements such as the Bolivarian Revolution in Venezuela are the progressive link between the popular revolution of the masses, and the communist revolution of the proletariat. In order to secure the latter, it's imperative that North American revolutionaries wishing to fulfill their anti-fascist and anti-imperialist responsibilities support the former critically, yet unconditionally. Without such transcontinental cooperation, it will be impossible to defeat capitalism and neo-colonialism in the Western Hemisphere. Neoliberalism must be defeated on a continental level.

c. Communism

No word utters confusion more than Communism. Especially since the collapse of the Soviet Union. However, the People's Republic of China (PRC)is proving this concept with rapid success. Deserts are being turned into grassland and forests. The PRC also has the world's largest robotics industry. No longer are the stereotypes of Communist Party-led societies being riddled with food shortages, pollution, and technological backwardness. It's already been established that socialism is *economic patriotism*. Communism, or **Marxism-Leninism**, is the application of all sciences to the country's political economy.

To understand Communism, it's necessary to comprehend in detail the founders, Karl Marx and Frederick Engels, and more importantly, their work - theoretical and practical. What separates Communism from other schools of socialist thought is the adherence to logic, logic based on science. Marxism isn't simply a more aggressive form of socialism, but rather it's the more sophisticated variant. Marxism isn't based on this or that great idea, but on the ground conditions of reality. To quote Frederick Engels:[31]

"To make a science of Socialism, it had first to be placed upon a real basis"

(Frederick Engels; *Socialism: Utopian and Scientific.*, Pg. 53)

The real basis can best be explained by Karl Marx himself in his *Critique of the Gotha Programme*:[32]

"Labour is *not the source* of all wealth. *Nature* is just as much the source of use values (and it is surely of such that material wealth consists!) as labour, which itself is the only manifestation of a force of nature, human labour power. The above phrase is to be found in all children's primers and is correct in so far as it is *implied* that labour is performed with the appurtenant subjects and instruments. But a socialist programme cannot allow such bourgeois phrases to pass over in silence the *conditions* that alone give them meaning.

Only in so far as man from the beginning behaves towards nature, the primary source of use values, therefore also of wealth."

(Karl Marx; *Critique of the Gotha Programme.*, Pgs. 8-9)

Why does this matter? It matters because the most rewarding tasks are also the most difficult. Anyone can fire rounds at bourgeois police or corporate lobbyists. Very few can teach the masses how to perform the functions of the society themselves. Again, why does this matter? It is due to the fact that the proletarians themselves have built the capitalist infrastructure: factories, fisheries, commercial ports, telecommunication networks, railways, and highways.

The workers built capitalism, yet they receive nothing from it on their terms. The socialization of production, meaning the market connecting all corners of the world into one money-making scheme, has set the precedent for the working class seizure of state power for two reasons:

a.) The increasing misery caused by the socially produced wealth of the world being allocated into the hands of a few monopoly capitalists has led to global turmoil in the form of a class war, and

b.) The instruments to operate a Communist-led state are already here to secure enough abundance for everyone's needs.

Long story short, capitalism has outlived its historic purpose, which was to destroy feudalism and create a modern industrial society.

Karl Marx said it best in his *Manifesto of the Communist Party:*[33]

"The immediate aim of the Communists is the same as that of all other proletarian parties: formation of the proletariat into a class, the overthrow of the bourgeois supremacy, conquest of political power by the proletariat."

(Karl Marx, Frederick Engels: *Manifesto of the Communist Party & Principles of Communism.*, Pg. 47)

His most famous and most important ideological heir, Vladimir Lenin, understood that the Communists can only get into power not merely through a violent, spontaneous, and chaotic bloodbath, but by out-organizing the enemy in the administration of civil society. Lenin understood that the best way to organize the whole of civil society is to first consolidate an organization of professional revolutionaries, or a **vanguard party**. In the modern sense, the vanguard party is a "party of a new type," meaning that it operates as a military unit. Rather than as a parliamentary force vying to opportunistically acquire votes just so it can grab government seats. This is made clear in Lenin's, *What is to be Done?*:[34]

> "If we begin with the solid foundation of a strong organization of revolutionaries, we can ensure the stability of the movement as a whole and carry out the aims both of Socialism and of the trade unions proper."

(Vladimir Lenin; *What is to be Done?*., Pg. 76)

Yet, the vanguard party is only one of many components of Lenin's contribution to Marxist thought.

His other main component is his analysis of modern-day imperialism, or the takeover of nations through the export of finance capital as opposed to an all-out invasion as in the days of Alexander the Great. This means that nations in today's era are taken over by currency as opposed to firepower, at least initially. For this reason, Lenin understood well how dangerous the contradictions of capitalism can become. This is especially true in the global development of wealthier countries exporting their hard currencies to underdeveloped or forcefully de-developed regions to boost the economies of the imperial core. Such looting of resources is secured via subsidiaries of corporations and banks lobbying comprador-capitalist politicians, who allow their country's resources to be exported to the imperial countries while their countrymen themselves barely have enough to eat.

This creates turmoil to the point where[35]:

> ". . .the contradiction between a handful of ruling "civilized" nations and the hundreds of millions of the colonial and dependent people's of the world. Imperialism is the most barefaced exploitation and the most inhumane oppression of hundreds of millions of people inhabiting the vast colonies and dependent countries.
>
> The growth of revolutionary movement in all colonies and dependent countries without exception clearly testifies to this fact. This circumstance is of importance for the proletariat in that it radically undermines the position of capitalism by converting the colonies and dependent countries from reserves of imperialism into reserves of the proletarian revolution."

(Joseph Stalin, The Foundations of Leninism., Pg. 6)

The flexible blueprint of a Marxist-Leninist state(s) must be the main objective of the Pan-American revolution. Without such a blueprint, the movement will be subjected to isolation and capitulation. In order to stop the revolutionary gains from becoming essentially defunct, it's imperative to buckle down and wage a protracted, yet tactical struggle against imperialism and capitalism, along with their birth child - fascism.

IV. Communists and the Labor Movement: A Two-Pronged Assault on Western Imperialism.

The conditions in the North American imperial core are as follows:

a.) a fascist continent undergoing refeudalization and deindustrialization (often in the name of "environmentalism"),

b.) an apartheid-esque regime(s) where the weakest links in the matrix of capitalism are the internal colonies (or areas of oppressed, exploited peoples within an advanced country's borders) of the United States and Canada.

Therefore, the avenue of struggle must be unique in and of itself. There must be a merger of parliamentary and *outside-the-box* measures to guarantee the proletarian seizure of state power. However, the main route of contention between the ruling classes and workers is the labor movement. This struggle is more universal than mathematical. Therefore, the liberation of oppressed nationalities and the working classes as a whole is tied together, since they both maintain the neoliberal world economic order - both from within and external to the North American imperial proper.

What is the correct and most decisive method of class conflict on behalf of the proletariat against the bourgeoisie? Only the combination of theory and practice, along with being knowledgeable about the general history of the movement, can win against the forces of plutocracy and privilege. Without this merger, the proletariat will lose to fascism. Deeper than that, the rapidly degenerating ecological situation will also push the working classes into extinction. Whether it be through depopulation, or genetic modification as is noted in the *Great Reset Agenda* laid out by the new generation of capitalists[36].

Why are they doing this? Automation has rendered the working classes obsolete to the modern-day, late-capitalist system. The concepts of nation, family, and sanity are being wiped away. Due to this fact, it's evident that the international class struggle will and must take the form of a patriotic struggle wherever the links in the capitalist world order are the most decayed and ready to burst.

UP WITH AMERICA!
UP WITH COMMUNISM!

ANNOTATED BIBLIOGRAPHY

1. "The United States appears to be destined by Providence to plague America with misery in the name of liberty." (Simon Bolivar, 1829)

2. "That whenever any Form of Government becomes destructive of these ends, it is the right of the People to alter or to abolish it, and to institute new Government, laying its foundation on such principles, and organizing its powers in such form, as to them shall seem most likely to effect their Safety and Happiness... it is their right, it is their duty, to throw off such Government, and to provide new Guards for their future security." (Thomas Jefferson, 1776)

3. Refeudalize, Refeudalization: A process of stunting, overhauling, and decreasing industrial and infrastructural development when it no longer becomes profitable. This causes mass unemployment and the overall criminalization of the working classes. Mass instability, lack of investment, and decapitated manufacturing forge a new generation of Capitalists who behave in a semi-feudal manner. Workers' protections are stripped away, both in public and private policy. These policies include being in perpetual debt to one's employer due to them taking advantage of their precarious situation, such as providing their workers with loaned shelter; undocumented migrant workers, etc. This social arraignment is protected and reinforced by the most medieval elements of that particular society, such as mega-churches led by religious fanatics, men's rights organizations, pro-prostitution lobbies, ultra-conservative death squads, armed vigilantes, nationalistic politicians, etc.

4. Neocolonial, Neocolonialism: The act of a larger, more developed country preying upon an oftentimes smaller, less developed country by taking over its production through exporting finance capital. The local subsidiaries of those who provide them with finance capital - the companies of the developed countries - will bankroll their countries' politicians into serving the interests of those who pay them, the capitalists of the developed countries. This means allowing the land, water, electricity, industrial, and all other wants and necessities of life to be put into the

hands of foreign corporations on a mass scale. These politicians often make "defense treaties" with the larger, more developed nations for "mutual protection" for "shared" interests. In reality, these put these "independent" countries at gunpoint mercy of the more developed country as their militaries are allowed to set up bases there. The only difference between neocolonialism and colonialism is that the former can change foreign masters.

5. Ortiz, R.D. (2014). *An Indigenous People's History of the United States* (Pgs. 15-16). Boston, Massachusetts: Beacon Press.

6. Retrieved from *CIA World Factbook* (CIA [dot] gov).

7. A region's violence is largely determined by the amount or lack of resources. If resources are scarce, then warfare will be common when abundance or surplus becomes a deficiency for public wants and needs. This has led to unusually cruel and authoritarian governments often based in areas with recalcitrant weather or meager amounts of natural resources, or most importantly, arable land.

8. Michael, Lev; Chousou-Polydouri, Natalia (2020). "Computational phylogenetics and the classification of South American language". *Language and Linguistics Compass*.

9. Ortiz, R.D. (2014). *An Indigenous People's History of the United States* (Pg. 16). Boston, Massachusetts: Beacon Press.

10. Mariaegui, J.C. (1928). *Siete Ensayos de la Interpretación de la Realidad Peruana* (Pg. 7). Lima, Peruo: Biblioteca Amauta.

11. Bacon's Rebellion was a unified effort on behalf of enslaved Africans and indentured whites against the colonial authorities in Virginia from 1676 to 1677. Although the intentions were ethically questionable due to the purpose of the upheaval being more indigenous lands, the overall tactics were centuries ahead of their time. For the purpose of safeguarding the longevity of colonial interests, the ruling aristocratic elites of the colonies began to draw the color line: indentured servitude was abolished and fully replaced by chattel slavery.

12. Zinn, H. (1980). *A People's History of the United States* (Pg. 5). London, England, and New York, United States: Longman.

13. Nkrumah, K. (2004). Neocolonialism: The Highest Stage of Imperialism (Pg. xiv). London, England: Panaf Books.

14. Mao, T.T. (1965). *Selected Works of Mao Tse-Tung Volume I* (Pg. 13). Peking, China: Foreign Language Press.

15. Shakur, S. (2004). *MONSTER: The Autobiography of an L.A. Gang Member* (Pgs. xi-xii). New York: Grove Press.

16. Retrieved from the *National Institute of Justice.*

17. Retrieved from *FixFamilyCourts* [dot] com.

18. The *Belt and Road* Initiative by the Marxist-Leninist government of the People's Republic of China is a drive towards sustainability, development, and the overall breaking of the neoliberal world order which relies on neocolonial frameworks of exploitation from the periphery to the imperial core in the West.

19. The North American states such as the US and Canada have to rely on imported foreign labor from the very same countries they exploit to sustain their domestic economies. One such example is the United States' shortage of engineers causing brain drain (or the practice of exporting a country's skilled labor) in the Third World being sponsored by multinational corporations.

20. Progressive Bolivia is an example of one such revitalization of national identity; reclaiming it from hundreds of years of colonialism. One such revitalization is establishing Bolivia as a plurinational republic (or a state where multiple nations coincide within a centralized administration while retaining an autonomous status). This has given indigenous people considerably more political and economic power, especially as Evo Morales has lifted their social position.

21. Stalin, J. (2020). *The Foundations of Leninism* (Pg. 6). Paris: Foreign Language Press.

22. Castro, F. (2007). *Fidel Castro Reader* (Pg. 293). New York: Ocean Press.

23. Socialism in simpler terms can be described as **economic patriotism** or an economy framed around the betterment of the nation's downtrodden as a whole over the market incentive. This includes the establishment of infrastructures such as roads, trams, railways, and canals, as well as bridges, refineries, and ports. Another way to frame socialism or economic patriotism is to say it's a policy of establishing secure investments for long-term growth over maximizing profits for short-term gain.

24. *"Counter-Terrorism"* measures on behalf of the North American imperialists along with their puppet governments south of the US-Mexican border are a means of suppressing any dissent to North American-led exploitation and plunder of Latin America's resources, as well as the anglophone Caribbean. Oftentimes, they'll recruit thugs and military careerists from Latin America, invite them to train at CIA-ran academies, and order them to infiltrate their home countries to cause havoc. This is the covert wing of the NATO deep-state.

25. After the United States and Canada leave NATO, independence must be granted to the main nations comprising the United States: New Afrikans in the Southeast, Chicanos in the Southwest, and Hawaiians and Puerto Ricans in their respective homelands as well. During such a process, the remnants of the United States and Canada are to merge into one plurinational republic or an administration where multiple nations coexist within the same state, yet retain their autonomous status. These multiple nations, once obtaining independence, must federate into one North American bulwark against fascism, racism, and imperialism. Such an administration is to become the People's Federation of America.

26. The Southwestern republic of the People's Federation of America, Aztlan, is to be reunified with Mexico with the sole intent of completing the North American Communist Revolution, from the North Pole and Greenland to the Yucatan. One administration would govern the whole of North America with one centralized economy. Such a measure would overall complete the defeat of fascism in the Western Hemisphere.

27. M, T.T. (1959). *Closing speech at the Second Session of the First National Committee of the Chinese People's Political Consultative Conference.*

28. The New Deal was a series of reforms meant to mitigate the effects of the Stock Market Crash of 1929 and the Great Depression (a global recession in the 1930s). These included social security, public infrastructure projects to employ millions, and the co-opting of unions to serve as a buffer between worker and owner while isolating the more recalcitrant elements of the labor movement.

29. Jackson, G. (1972). *Blood In My Eye* (Pg. 138). New York: Random House.

30. Lenin, V. (2021). *Left-Wing Communism: An Infantile Disorder* (Pg. 2020). Paris: Foreign Language Press.

31. Engels, F. (2020). *Socialism: Utopian and Scientific* (Pg. 53). Paris: Foreign Language Press.

32. Marx, K. (1972). *Critique of the Gothe Programme* (Pgs. 8-9). Peking: Foreign Languages Press.

33. Marx, K; Engels, F. (2020). *Manifesto of the Communist Party & Principles of Communism* (Pg. 47). Paris: Foreign Language Press.

34. Lenin, V. (1902). *What is to be Done?* (Pg. 76). Amazon Edition.

35. Stalin, J. (2020). *The Foundations of Leninism* (Pg. 6). Paris: Foreign Language Press.

36. *The Great Reset* Agenda is a globalized, fascist agenda to finish the refeudalization of the world due to regular capitalism being too unaffordable. This includes depopulation, sterilization, gentrification, deindustrialization, transhumanism, etc.